Natural Defenses

by Sandy Damashek

Table of Contents

CHAPTER 1

Ouch! Getting the Point

Plants and animals have natural ways to protect themselves. These are called natural **defenses**. Some plants and animals share the same kinds of defenses. They may have sharp growths, **poison**, or a bad smell.

Sharp growths that can poke and stick are good for keeping hungry animals away. You probably already know about some plants and animals that have this kind of defense.

Plant Spines, Prickles, and Thorns

What if you were a hungry burro trotting through the desert? Would a cactus look like a tasty meal? No way! Most kinds of cactus plants have stiff, sharp **spines**. These spines keep most animals from nibbling at the plant. Spines are an almost perfect defense system!

Prickly pear cactus

How do you think the hedgehog defends itself?

Other plants, such as thistles, have **prickles** instead of spines. Prickles are sharp growths on the "skin" of the plant. These prickles protect the flowers. Unlike spines, prickles are not plant leaves. Instead,

These sharp points on a rose stem are really prickles, not thorns.

they grow on leaves or other parts of a plant. Most people say that roses have thorns. Yet roses really have prickles.

A **thorn** is a kind of stem that grows out from the branches of the plant. Thorns are usually stiff and sharp. Blackberry and raspberry bushes have thorns. Some trees, such as honey locust trees, have thorns, too.

Spines, prickles, and thorns on plants send a clear message to hungry animals: Stay away!

Thorns make picking raspberries tricky!

Animal Spines (and We Don't Mean Backbones!)

Some animals have spines to protect them.

Porcupines have up to 30,000 sharp **quills**. When a porcupine is threatened, it spins around and swings its tail at its attacker. Each time the tail makes contact, quills come off. These quills go into the attacking animal's skin. They have barbs, which are like little hooks. The barbs hold tightly and the quills go deeper, sometimes causing death.

The porcupine's quills even keep this lion away!

Hedgehogs are little animals native to Europe, Africa, and Asia, but not North America. Hedgehogs and porcupines are related to each other, but not identical. Hedgehog spines do not come out easily. They are also not barbed.

Take a look at this hedgehog! By curling up into a ball, it is protecting its soft face, belly, and legs from **predators**. Hedgehogs curl up when they are defending themselves and when they are sleeping.

A hedgehog curls up in a ball for protection from predators.

CHAPTER 2

Poison Power

Poison is one of the best plant and animal defenses. Sometimes it causes an animal to become sick. Other times, it stops a predator dead in its tracks!

Zapped by Sap

Have you ever had poison ivy? Brushing against the leaves of the poison ivy plant can be all it takes for poison ivy sap to get on your arms or legs.

The sap from poison ivy has a chemical called urushiol. This chemical flows through the leaves, twigs, and roots of the poison ivy plant. When a poison ivy leaf touches your skin, urushiol causes a rash or blisters to form.

Poison Ivy   Poison Oak   Poison Sumac

Deadly Flowers, Seeds, and Berries

Animals can get sick from eating plants that have poison. They can even die. Most animals learn to stay away from plants that make them sick—and to keep their babies away, too. These animals cannot make a mistake.

Poisonous

Berries	Flowers	Seeds
Jasmine	Lily of the valley	Wild cherry
Mistletoe	Buttercup	Castor bean
Moonseed	Foxglove	Wisteria

Tiny But Deadly

It is no surprise that animals use poison as a defense, too.

Tiny poison arrow frogs from South America are about the size of a person's thumbnail. You might think that these frogs would be a perfect meal for animals in the rain forest. No way! They are some of the most poisonous animals of all. Poison oozes through their skin. It is a colorful sight, but a deadly one. The bright colors of these frogs warn other animals to stay away.

Get the Point?

The Choco Indians of South America dip their arrows in poison arrow frog poison before they go hunting.

The bright color of this tiny poison arrow frog is a warning.

Bad Bites

Many snakes shoot their poison through their fangs! To inject their poison, snakes have to bite into the skin of other animals. The snake poison, called **venom**, travels through the hollow fangs into the wounds. It can paralyze an animal and even cause death.

The rattlesnake is one of four kinds of venomous snakes in the United States.

Spitting Snakes

Some snakes do not have to bite. Their fangs point forward so they can spit their venom to blind their enemies!

Poisonous Points

As if one defense isn't enough, many underwater creatures have double protection—poison and spines!

Check out this stonefish. It would win a contest for being the most poisonous fish. If its spines cut into another creature's skin, poisonous venom flows into the wound. The enemy can die in less than an hour.

Stonefish

Remember the Name

The names say it all. Like the stonefish, these animals have poisonous spines. A run-in with one of them will leave painful memories.

Long-spined sea urchin

Crown-of-thorns starfish

CHAPTER 3

What's That Smell?

So far, we have met spine-wearers and poison-bearers. Now it's time to meet the stinkers—plants and animals that give off bad odors!

Smelly Plants

Plants give off bad smells for two reasons. Some plant smells keep animals away. For example, Copper Canyon daisies smell like medicine. Their scent keeps deer from nibbling on their leaves and flowers.

Copper Canyon daisy

A Helpful Smell

The smell of a citronella plant keeps mosquitoes and other insects away. People use citronella candles for bite-free backyards.

When Bad Smells Are Good Smells

As strange as it may sound, certain plants use bad smells to attract animals.

The corpse flower is the world's largest—and perhaps smelliest—flower! Some people think it smells like rotten eggs when it blooms. Other people say it smells like a dead elephant. You get the picture. It smells bad!

Still, certain beetles love the corpse flower's smell. They flock to the blooming plant. When they do, they pollinate the flowers. This means that there will be new corpse plants (just as smelly as the old ones).

This corpse flower is big and smelly!

Animal Stinkers

The word *skunk* probably makes you wrinkle your nose. When skunks are threatened, they turn around, put their tail in the air, and spray! Both males and females give off the odor. If you have ever smelled a skunk, you will never forget it.

Stinkbugs are small but smelly. Their odor drives away many predators looking for a bug lunch. Like all defenses a bad smell usually tells animals to stay away!

The Best Defense

So, what is the best defense? It depends. Plants and animals develop the best defense for their habitat and the predators they share it with. Clearly, sharp spines, prickles, thorns, poison, and bad smells suit some plants and animals just fine!

The skunk's raised tail is a signal: Stay away!

Glossary

defense *(di-FENS)* a way that a plant or an animal protects itself *(page 2)*

poison *(POY-zuhn)* something harmful when taken into the body *(page 2)*

predator *(PRED-uh-tuhr)* an animal that eats other animals *(page 6)*

prickle *(PRIK-uhl)* a small, sharp point on plant stems, leaves, or flowers *(page 4)*

quill *(KWIL)* a stiff, sharp spine on a porcupine or hedgehog *(page 5)*

spines *(SPIGHNZ)* stiff, sharp growths on a plant or an animal *(page 3)*

thorn *(THAWRN)* a kind of plant stem that is thin, hard, and sharp *(page 4)*

venom *(VEN-uhm)* a poison produced by an animal *(page 10)*

Index

Comprehension Check

Summarize

Use a Venn diagram to tell how two animals or plants from the book are the same and different. Then summarize the information.

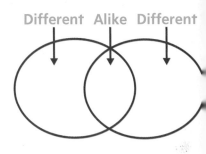

Think and Compare

1. Reread pages 5–6. How are porcupines and hedgehogs the same? How are they different? **(Compare and Contrast)**

2. What was the most interesting fact in the book? Tell why it was interesting. **(Analyze)**

3. Why is it important for people to learn how plants and animals protect themselves? **(Evaluate)**